ORIGAMI
FESTIVALS

Chinese New Year

Robyn Hardyman

W
FRANKLIN WATTS
LONDON • SYDNEY

Franklin Watts
First published in Great Britain in 2016 by The Watts Publishing Group

Credits
Series Editors: Sarah Eason and Jennifer Sanderson
Series Designer: Jessica Moon
All origami photography by Jessica Moon

Picture credits: Cover: Shutterstock: Comodo777, Redberry. Inside: Shutterstock:
Asharkyu 12-13, ChameleonsEye 7, Fotohunter 18-19, Kongsky 25b, Redberry
4t, Stripped Pixel 13, Szefei 19, WeStudio 25t, Yurumi 67.

Every attempt has been made to clear copyright. Should there be any inadvertent
omission please apply to the publisher for rectification.

HB ISBN: 978 1 4451 5075 8
PB ISBN: 978 1 4451 5076 5

Printed in China

Franklin Watts
An imprint of
Hachette Children's Group
Part of The Watts Publishing Group
Carmelite House
50 Victoria Embankment
London EC4Y 0DZ

An Hachette UK Company
www.hachette.co.uk

www.franklinwatts.co.uk

Contents

Chinese New Year

Chinese New Year is the biggest Chinese festival of the year. The date of the festival changes each year. This is because the Chinese set festival dates using a calendar based on the movements of the Moon. Chinese New Year always falls between 21 January and 21 February, on the date of the **new Moon** closest to the beginning of spring in China.

Red lanterns are **symbols** of luck and wealth, and you will see them hanging everywhere at Chinese New Year. People hang them in their homes and in the streets to ensure good luck.

Celebrate!

Folds, Bases and Paper

These instructions explain the main folds and bases you will use. The activities are rated from 1 to 5 to show level of difficulty.

Valley fold: To make a valley fold, fold the paper towards you.

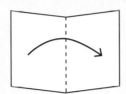

Mountain fold: To make a mountain fold, fold the paper away from you.

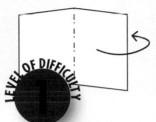

LEVEL OF DIFFICULTY 1

 Turn over the model

 Rotate the model

Cut with scissors

Push or pull in this direction

Square Base

 1   2   3   4

 5   6  7 8

Bird Base: Start with a square base.

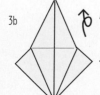 1   2 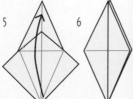 3a

3b 4 5 6

These festivals very widely celebrated. In China it is a **public holiday** and it lasts for three days. The celebrations, though, can go on for two weeks. People celebrate at home with their families and friends. They prepare the house and eat special foods. They also join in with public celebrations in the streets, such as dancing and fireworks.

In this book you will find out how to make some wonderful origami pieces that will make your festival even more fun!

Waterbomb Base

 1   2 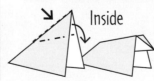 3 4

 5   5a   6

Inside/Outside Reverse Folds

 Inside   Outside

Squash Fold

 1 2 3 4

Paper: You can use almost any kind of paper, but you can also buy origami paper from craft shops.

The Animals of the Zodiac

The Chinese calendar is made up of a cycle of 12 years. Each year is named after an animal. People believe that if they are born in the year of a particular animal, they will have some of the **characteristics** of that animal.

The Animals

The 12 animals in the Chinese **zodiac** are: rat, ox, dragon, monkey, snake, rooster, tiger, horse, goat, dog, rabbit and pig. The story behind the animals of the zodiac is that the **Jade Emperor** of China set up a race for all animals across a fast-flowing river. The first 12 animals to cross the river would have a year named after them. The kind ox carried the cat and the rat. The rat pushed the cat off and was first to jump to the bank and have a year named after it. The ox was second. The rabbit crossed on stepping stones and the goat, monkey and rooster crossed on a raft.

2008, 2020

2009, 2021

2010, 2022

2011, 2023

2012, 2024

2013, 2025

牛 虎 兔 龙

鼠

蛇

木 水

The order of the zodiac animals reflects the order they finished the race. The rat was first and the boar was last.

6

Different Qualities

The goat is creative, the rooster is hard-working and the dog is honest. The rat is **ambitious**, the tiger likes to take **risks**, the snake is wise and the horse is independent. The ox is a leader, the rabbit is **affectionate**, the monkey is clever and the pig is willing to share.

2007, 2019

2006, 2018

2005, 2017

2004, 2016

2015, 2027

2014, 2026

Lucky Dragon

The dragon is the luckiest zodiac animal, so the year of the dragon is the best one to be born in. People born in this year are hard-working and successful, and good at encouraging others to succeed. They also love to have fun.

Friendly Pig

Make this cute origami pig to decorate your home.
The pig is peaceful, friendly and honest – but untidy!

LEVEL OF DIFFICULTY
2

1 Start with your paper colour side down. Mountain fold your paper in half, and then unfold.

2 Valley fold the top and bottom of your paper into the centre.

3 Valley fold all four corners into the centre of your model.

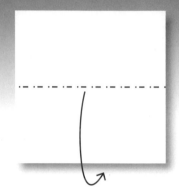
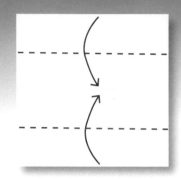
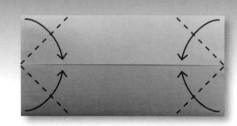

4 Valley fold the left and right sides into the centre and then unfold.

5 Unfold the four corner folds made in step 3.

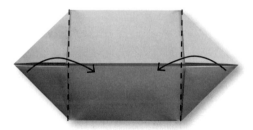

6 Valley fold the top left layer, flattening the corner as you go, to perform a squash fold.

7 Repeat step 6 on the remaining three corners.

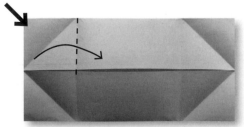

Close-up of
squash fold

8

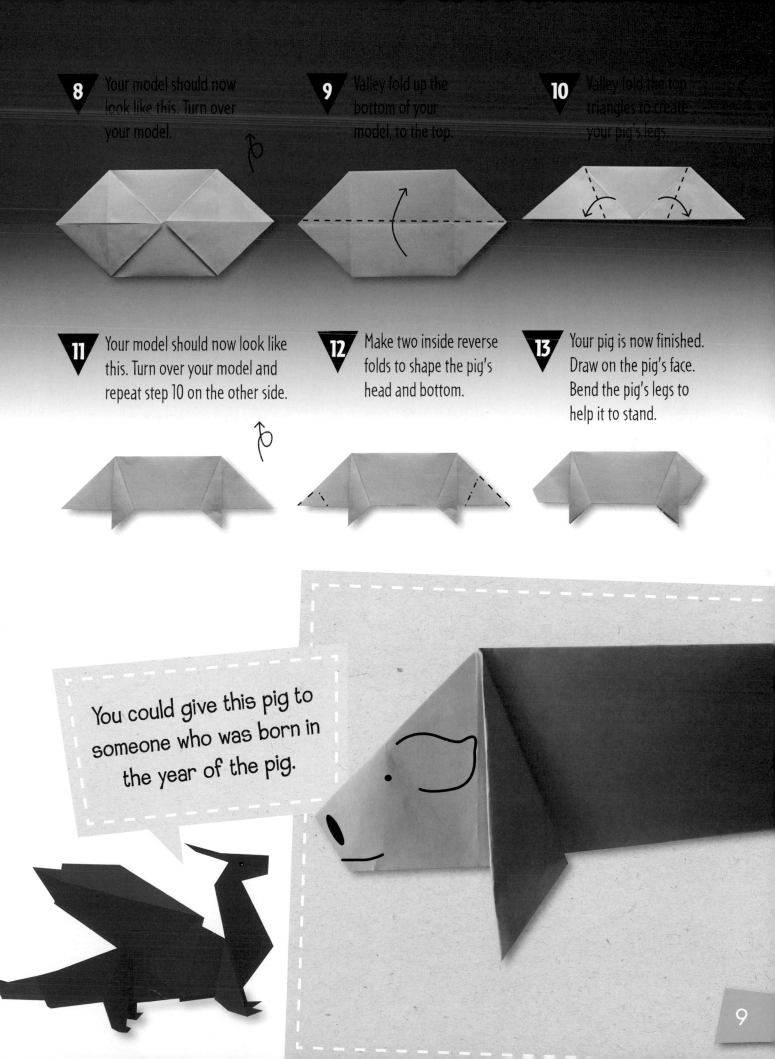

8 Your model should now look like this. Turn over your model.

9 Valley fold up the bottom of your model, to the top.

10 Valley fold the top triangles to create your pig's legs.

11 Your model should now look like this. Turn over your model and repeat step 10 on the other side.

12 Make two inside reverse folds to shape the pig's head and bottom.

13 Your pig is now finished. Draw on the pig's face. Bend the pig's legs to help it to stand.

You could give this pig to someone who was born in the year of the pig.

Charming Snake

Make this fun, festive snake! The snake is charming, clever and patient.

1 Start with your paper colour side down. Valley fold your paper in half.

2 Valley fold the top layer of your paper about one-tenth of the way up.

3 Mountain fold the top layer back the same amount.

4 Repeat steps 2 and 3, keeping the folds even, until you reach the centre of your paper.

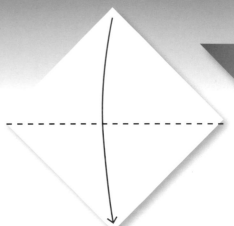

5 Your model should now look like this. Turn over your model.

6 Repeat steps 2 to 4 on the reverse.

7 Open the left end slightly, then make an outside reverse fold to create the snake's head.

8 Make another outside reverse fold to shape the head.

9 Make an inside reverse fold to finish your head.

Close-up of head

10 Valley-fold and mountain-fold the body along its length to give it shape.

11 Your model is now finished. Open the head slightly to give your snake extra shape. Smooth the body folds with your fingers to create a curvy body.

Cut and stick a red tongue to your snake's mouth. Don't forget to draw some eyes on its face.

Getting Ready

It is important for everything to be ready for the beginning of a new year. People clean their homes thoroughly and decorate them. This is to remove all traces of bad luck from the old year, and to make the home beautiful and ready to receive good luck in the new year.

These golden boats are called *yuanbao*. They contain golden money and are symbols of wealth.

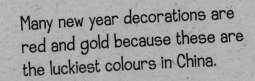

Many new year decorations are red and gold because these are the luckiest colours in China.

Bringing Good Fortune

The decorations are designed to bring good luck. Red also frightens off a monster called Nian who visits on New Year's Eve, and gold brings wealth. There are also lots of fish decorations. The Chinese word for 'fish' sounds like the word for 'plenty', so people hang fish decorations to bring them wealth in the year to come. Goldfish are popular because of their colour. Fruit flower blossoms are also used as decorations, to bring a good crop **harvest** in the new year.

Good luck!

Chun Lian (Decorations)

On New Year's Eve, people hang strips of red paper on either side of their front door. **Verses** are written on them in beautiful writing. The verses tell of the happy new year that is to come. These decorations are called *chun lian*.

Decorating Homes

Homes are richly decorated on the outside with strings of lights, and lanterns are hung everywhere. These light the way for the family's kitchen **god**, who travels to see the Jade Emperor. The Jade Emperor can send good luck to the family. People also hang bunches of **firecrackers** outside. These are similar to fireworks, and their loud bangs scare away any bad luck.

13

Fruit Flower Blossom

The pretty peach blossom is a symbol of long life, romance and success.

1 Start with your paper colour side down. Valley fold your paper in half from top to bottom.

2 Valley fold the left side over to the right, then unfold.

3 Valley fold the left side over to the right, about two-thirds of the way down the left side.

4 Valley fold the right side over to the left.

5 Valley fold your model in half from left to right.

6 Cut the bottom of your model in an arc shape.

7 Your model should now look like this. Open out your model.

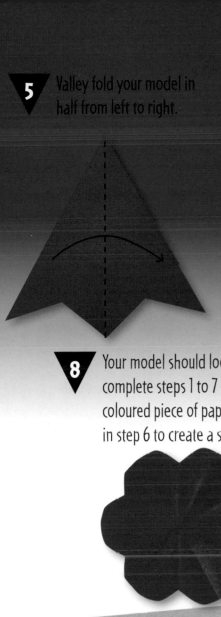

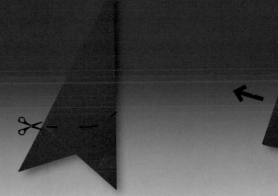

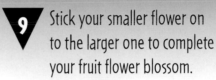

8 Your model should look like this. Now complete steps 1 to 7 with a different coloured piece of paper. Cut away more in step 6 to create a smaller flower.

9 Stick your smaller flower on to the larger one to complete your fruit flower blossom.

Peach blossoms are symbols of romance so they are popular with people who are looking for love!

Goldfish

The goldfish is another symbol of wealth and success. Make a lot in gold or orange paper. Hang them up to bring you luck in the year to come!

1 Start with your paper coloured side down. Valley fold down the top to the bottom.

2 Valley fold the left and right sides of your paper into the centre.

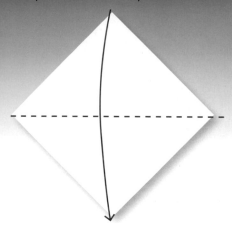

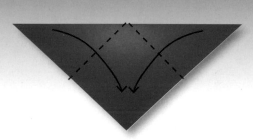

3 Valley fold up the two top layers.

4 Valley fold the top layers again, to the sides.

5 Valley fold up the upper layer of the bottom of your model.

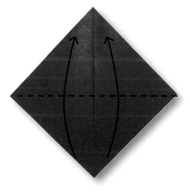

6 Again, valley fold up the upper layer of the bottom of your model.

7 Mountain fold back the bottom of your model.

8 Push the left and right sides together so that your model opens along the bottom edge. Keep pushing them together until you have flattened your model.

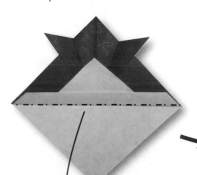

9 Your model should now look like this. Valley fold the right side and then unfold.

10 Open and unfold your model so it looks like it did at the start of step 7.

11 Cut the left and right edges of the back layer, then repeat steps 7 and 8.

12 Your model should now look like this. Make an inside reverse fold to the right side.

13 Fold back the upper layer on the right side to create your goldfish's tail.

14 Your goldfish is now complete. Give the tail shape by cutting or folding it so it has a curved edge.

For a colourful display, make lots of these fish in different patterned papers.

New Year's Day

At midnight on New Year's Eve, people set off firecrackers to scare away evil **spirits**. On New Year's Day, families gather to enjoy a feast and to celebrate. They eat special foods, such as little **dumplings** with a garlic and **soy sauce**. A coin is hidden inside one dumpling, and it brings luck to the person who finds it. Food is also prepared for the spirits of **ancestors**, because people believe they are present at the holiday.

Lucky dragons, flowers and firecrackers are popular decorations at Chinese New Year.

18

Kung Hei Fat Choy

Family and friends gather on New Year's Day. They greet each other with the words 'Kung hei fat choy'. These words mean Happy New Year!

Presents For Children

Chinese children are given a present by their family on New Year's Day. This is a red envelope called a *Hong Bao*. It contains sweets or money. It is thought to be rude to open your *Hong Bao* in front of the person who gives it to you. After the meal, families play games and sing songs together. They often then go out to join in with the public festivities, and to visit other families and friends.

Have fun!

Chopstick Wrapper

Many Chinese foods are eaten with chopsticks. This chopstick wrapper would make a lovely gift for friends and family.

1 Start with your paper colour side down. Valley fold your paper in half and then unfold.

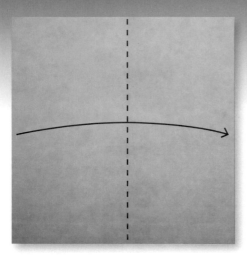

2 Valley fold the left and right sides into the centre. Unfold the paper.

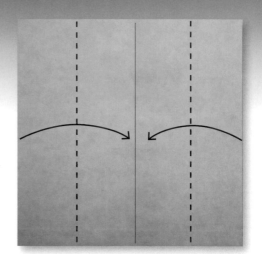

3 Valley fold the two top corners.

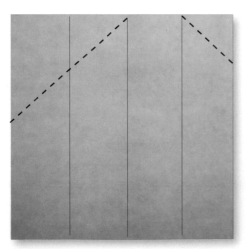

4 Valley fold the right side into the centre.

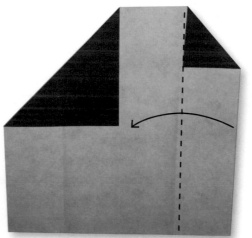

5 Valley fold the left side over to the right.

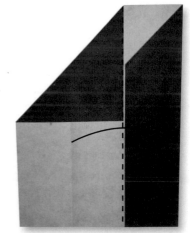

6 Valley fold the model behind your model.

7 Mountain fold the bottom of your model to stop your chopsticks falling out.

8 Your chopstick wrapper is now complete.

Make these chopstick wrappers from different pretty papers to make your table look festive.

Gold Nugget

This gorgeous nugget of gold might bring you wealth in the new year.

1 Valley fold up the bottom of your paper a distance of about one-eighth.

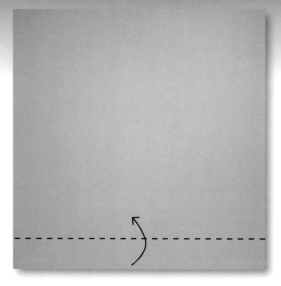

2 Valley fold the top down to the bottom.

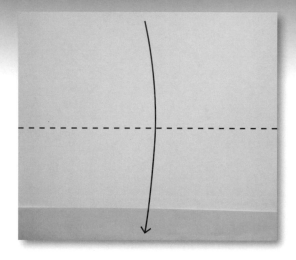

3 Valley fold the left and right corners.

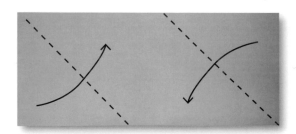

4 Rotate and turn over your model.

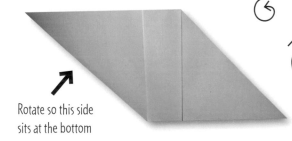

Rotate so this side sits at the bottom

5 Valley fold your model in half from top to bottom.

6 Valley fold the right side and tuck into the left triangle pocket.

7 Mountain fold the left side and tuck it into the triangle pocket on the reverse.

8 Your nugget is now finished. To give it shape and help it stand up, insert your fingers to smooth and open the bottom of your model.

Make a lot of these nuggets to bring you good fortune in the year ahead.

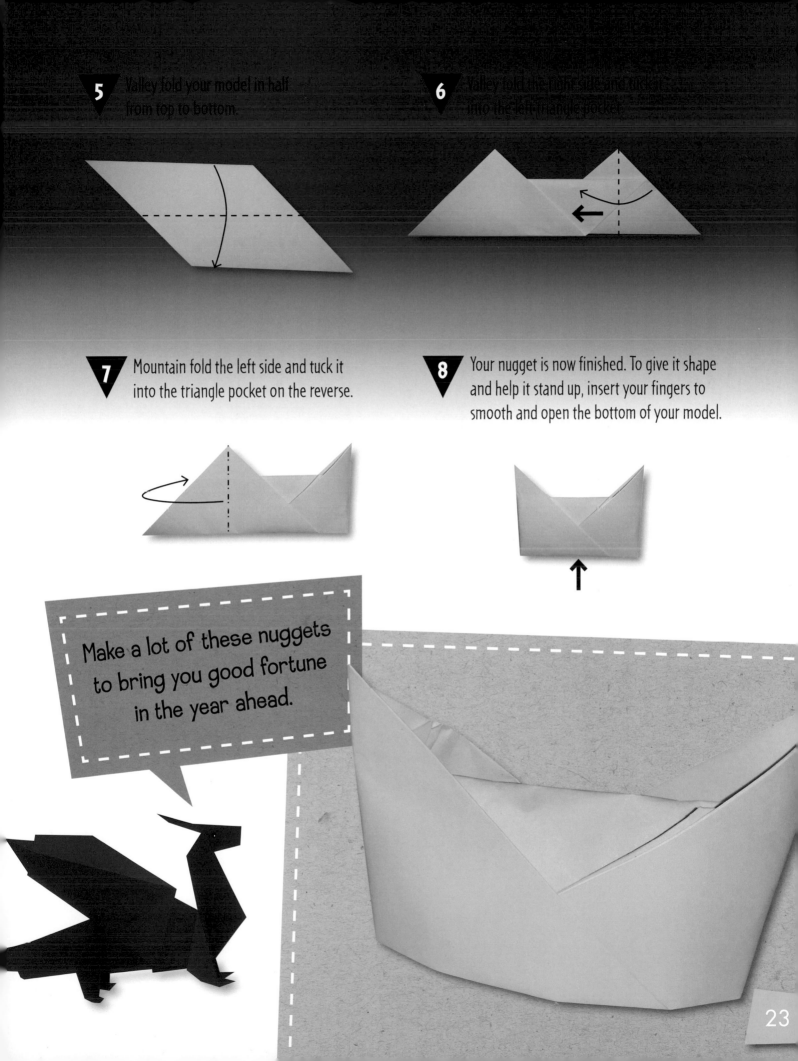

23

Street Celebrations

Celebrate!

The street celebrations for Chinese New Year are very noisy and colourful. Happy crowds gather to watch skilled performers do **traditional** dances to the beat of drums, **cymbals** and a **gong**.

The Dancing Lion

The Lion Dance is to bring good luck. It is performed by two dancers. One is inside the lion's head. Another is in its body. Together, they dance through the streets looking for green leaves hung above doorways. Packets of money are inside the leaves. The lion finds the leaves and scatters them on the ground as a symbol of a fresh start. The lion meets a 'Laughing **Buddha**', dressed as a monk (a holy man). He wears a robe and a mask. The Buddha teases the lion with a fan made of banana leaves. This makes the lion jump around in an amazing acrobatic dance.

Friendly Dragons

The Dragon Dance is another traditional part of New Year. For the Chinese, dragons are helpful and friendly, not scary. They bring long life and wisdom. The dragon in the dance is a colourful, long puppet raised on poles. It is moved by performers who raise and lower the poles to make the dragon dance. It snakes through the streets, chasing away evil spirits.

Festival of Lanterns

The Festival of Lanterns takes place on the fifteenth day of celebrations. The streets are decorated with red lanterns of all sizes, and there is music and dancing. Some of the lanterns have riddles written on them, for people to guess the answers.

When the Dragon Dance is performed at night, blazing torches are carried to light the way. It is a truly spectacular display.

Lucky Dragon

This lovely dragon can bring good luck to your Chinese New Year.

1 Start with your base. Valley fold the two top edges into the centre.

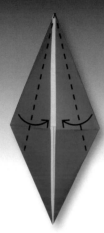

2 Valley fold the right side over to the left. Turn over your model.

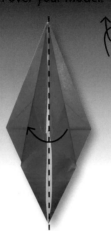

3 Valley fold down the top piece.

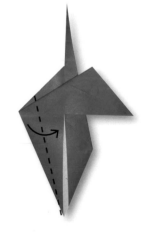

4 Valley fold the right side over to the left.

5 Valley fold up the upper bottom layer.

6 Valley fold down the top piece.

7 Valley fold the top left side into the centre.

8 Valley and mountain fold the first wing and make a **concertina fold**.

9 Your model should now look like this. Turn over your model.

26

14 Your model should now look like this. Rotate the model by 90 degrees clockwise.

15 Make three inside reverse folds to shape the neck and head.

3 2 1

Close-up of head folds

16 Open out the bottom part to help your model stand. Your dragon is finished.

This dragon will get your new year off to a great start!

Lantern

You can make your Chinese lantern in many bright colours, but remember that the luckiest colour is red!

1 Start with a waterbomb base. Valley fold the upper left and right sides into the centre.

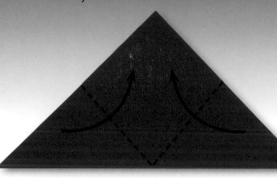

2 Your model should now look like this. Turn over your model.

3 Repeat the valley folds from step 1 on this side.

4 Valley fold the top left and right sides into the centre.

5 Valley fold up the top layer of the top points, and slot them into the pockets of the side flaps you just created.

Close-up of points going into pocket slots

6 Your model should now look like this. Turn it over and repeat steps 4 and 5 on the reverse.

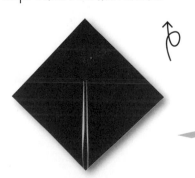

7 Your model should now look like this. Blow gently into the small hole at the bottom to inflate your lantern. Carefully pull out the sides to flatten it... finely fold them.

8 Your lantern is now finished. Make a few more and thread some string through them to hang them up.

Blow here

Long strings of these beautiful lanterns will make your home look so pretty for the new year!

Glossary

affectionate showing feelings of fondness

ambitious having a strong need to be successful

ancestors members of a person's family who have died

Buddha a thinker who started a religion called Buddhism

characteristics qualities that form part of a person's character

concertina fold a type of fold used in origami that is sometimes called a zig-zag fold or an accordion fold. The folds are alternatively made to the front and back in zig-zag folds

cymbals musical instruments made of metal plates that are hit to make sounds

dumplings balls of dough that are cooked

firecrackers small and loud fireworks designed to make noise rather than light

god a male spirit or being that has great power, strength and knowledge

gong a musical instrument that is a large metal disc. It that makes an echoing sound when it is hit

harvest the season for gathering crops

Jade Emperor the first god according to traditional Chinese tales

new Moon the time when the Moon looks like a narrow crescent that is going to wax (increase) to a full Moon

public holiday a holiday for a whole country

risks chances that may lead to losses

soy sauce a salty sauce that is made from soya beans and is used in Chinese cooking

spirits beings that cannot be seen

symbols signs that are used to represent something

traditional done often or regularly at a certain time of year

verses poems

zodiac an area of sky divided into 12 equal parts, each with a name

Further Reading

Books

Chinese Fairytales, Sun Xuegang and Cai Guoyun, Puffin

Chinese New Year (Festivals Around the World), Grace Jones, BookLife

The Great Race: The Story of the Chinese Zodiac, Dawn Casey, Barefoot Books Ltd

Websites

This website has a lot of information on Chinese New Year. Log on to:
www.dkfindout.com/us/more-find-out/festivals-and-holidays/chinese-new-year

For facts and fun on Chinese New Year, including games, go to:
www.topmarks.co.uk/chinesenewyear/chinesenewyear.aspx

There are many activities on Chinese New Year at this website:
www.activityvillage.co.uk/chinese-new-year

Note to parents and teachers
Every effort has been made by the Publisher to ensure that these websites contain no inappropriate or offensive material. However, because of the nature of the Internet, it is impossible to guarantee that the contents of these sites will not be altered. We strongly advise that Internet access is supervised by a responsible adult.

Index